Get Your Skates On!

Written by
Cath Jones

Illustrated by
James Hearne

Eve's back yard was full of ramps and slopes. She had made them from bits and pieces people had thrown out.

It looked like a proper skate park!

"You're a fantastic skater," her mum said.

"Do you think I could join the skating club?" Eve asked.

"Have belief in your skills, Eve," Mum told her.

Eve turned up early at Skate Club.

"Welcome," said a man. "I'm Coach."

Just then, a boy sped down a slope and jumped into the air.

"Well done, Pete!" shouted Coach.

Pete's good, Eve thought.

Now it was Eve's turn. She jumped from ramp to ramp and completed everything really quickly.

Coach grinned. "You're good!" he said to Eve. "Would you like to enter a skating contest with us?"

The next day, Pete appeared at Eve's back gate. He was impressed!

"Wow! Your yard is like a skate park!" he said. "Can I skate with you? We could be a team."

So Eve taught Pete some bold stunts and he taught her some clever tricks.

"We're a fantastic team," said Pete. "We might win the contest and get the prize money."

On the day of the contest, Eve's mum drove Eve and Pete in her car. They had plenty of time to get there.

But the trip went very slowly. They got totally stuck in traffic.

"We need to hurry," said Pete.

"Why don't we get out and skate to the contest?" Eve said. "If we hurry, we might just make it in time. It's worth trying!"

Quickly, they put on their skates.

Eve and Pete raced along the path.

They spotted lots of skate club members who were stuck in the traffic jam too.

"Come and join us!" Eve yelled to them. "We'll get there quicker."

Soon, the whole skate club was skating to the contest.

But time was running out.

"Let's take a shortcut," Pete yelled.

They raced down an alley, but now there was lots of stuff in their way!

Eve had to jump a shopping trolley.

People clapped and cheered as the skaters sped past.

When they got there, the hall where the contest was being held was all locked up.

"Oh no! We must be too late," Eve said.

"Let's go home," said Pete.

But just then, a reporter ran up to them.

"Your skating is fantastic!" she yelled. "I saw you flying through the air! Will you skate for me now? I will film you."

That night, Eve and Pete watched the skating contest on the news. Then they watched the reporter's film of them skating in the street.

Now they were all stars!

Ransom Reading Stars Phonics Phase 5 titles

Neat and Clean
Stunt Star
Three Clues
The Royal Chopper
Flip Flap Fox
Little Phantom
Eric the Pie Rat
Meet the Dolphins
Airship Rescue
Caves
The Floating Markets of Bangkok
Looking at the Stars
Canute's Flute
Mudlarking
The Clink Clank Clunk
Spot the Magnets
Planets are Spheres
Hunting for the Northern Lights
Mr White's Whiskers
The Cunning Plan
Living in the Best Homes
Camping Kit
Games We Can Play
The King's Cats
Luke and the Mule

Dazzling Water Sports
Who Needs Water?
Keeping Water Clean
Ships and Boats
Look at My Tail
Willow Saves the Day
The Scooter Contest
Wild Weather
Stone Soup
The Singing Chef

Celest and the Crystal Bracelet
The Tap Tap Kids
Fantastic Frogs
Jogging into Space

Bridges
The Adventure of the Sunken Gold
Sir Jeff's Birthday Treat
Shipwrecks
The Magic Clog Dancer
Skipper Kipper and the Treasure Chest
A Peanut Butter Treat
Different Kinds of Music
Monkey Mischief
Let's Visit South Africa
Climbing
Getting to Gran's
We Need Bees!
Joe's Gold
The Moon Bean
A Messy Mystery
The Lady with the Lamp
Let's Go Running
Ten Shed Fred
Foolish Ostrich
Get Your Skates On!
Telephones
Going by Bus
Tweet, Tweet, Parp!
Fire
The Fire of London
The Elephant's Child
Bikes Then and Now
The Best Nest

Fruit!
Travel and Transport
Bears
A Very Special Musician

Foxes
Farmer Flo's Happy Cows
The Frog in the Well
The Biggest Carrot in the World
Magical Creatures
"We Are Not Monkeys!"
How Will You Get There?
The Nest Quest
Ella's Dragon
Flutter By, Butterfly!
The Princess and the Pea
Space Flight
Fantastic Feet!
Muscat: Our City, Our Home
A Monster under the Bed
Spider Girl
The Moon Race
Explorers Past and Present
Changes: Heating and Cooling
Hide and Peek
Volcanoes
The Rubbish Robot
Jake the Snake
"I'm Not a Monster!"

A full-colour A1 poster is available, showing all the books in the Reading Stars Phonics programme, together with details of what each book covers. Contact Ransom for a free copy.

Get Your Skates On!

Letters and Sounds Phase 5
Introduces alternative spellings for the phonemes: /ee/ (these, happy, chief, key)

Word count **435**

This book uses letters and sounds and common exception words that are found in Phases 2, 3 and 4 plus, from Phase 5, new graphemes for reading and alternative pronunciations of known graphemes for reading. It also uses the following from Phase 5:

Alternative spellings for the phonemes:
/ch/ (catch), **/u/** (some), **/i/** (happy, donkey), **/ear/** (beer), **/ar/** (father), **/air/** (there), **/or/** (all, four, caught), **/ur/** (learn, word), **/oo/** (could, put), **/ai/** (day, came), **/ee/** (sea, these, happy, chief, key)

Common exception words: **oh**, **their**, **people**, **looked**, **asked**, **where**, **who**, **thought**, **through**

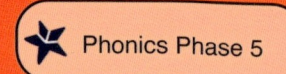 Phonics Phase 5